I0816327

# FUNKY-FEATURED DINOSAURS

Written by Rosie Rowntree

Illustrated by Marina Halak

First published in 2026 by Hungry Tomato Ltd
F15, Old Bakery Studios, Blewetts Wharf, Malpas Road, Truro, Cornwall,
TR1 1QH, UK.



A CIP catalog record for this book is available from the British Library.

ISBN 9781835696651

Manufactured in the USA

Discover more at
www.hungrytomato.com

HUNGRY
TOMATO®

# CONTENTS



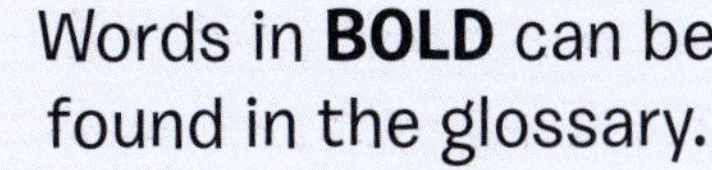
Words in **BOLD** can be found in the glossary.

# THE WORLD OF DINOSAURS

**Get ready to explore the wonderful world of dinosaurs! From the tiny Yanornis to the giant Nigersaurus, there are so many different types of dinosaurs to discover.**

## WHAT WERE THE DINOSAURS?

Dinosaurs were a group of **reptiles** that lived on Earth millions upon millions of years ago. They ranged in size from the from the cat-sized Sinosauropteryx to the building-sized Giraffatitan. The word "dinosaur" comes from two Greek words meaning "terrible" and "lizard".

## WHEN DID THE DINOSAURS LIVE?

Dinosaurs lived on Earth for almost 180 million years. But they didn't all live at the same time! Some were around later than others. Scientists think that the earliest dinosaurs first appeared over 245 million years ago, while the last roamed the Earth 66 million years ago.

## WHAT HAPPENED TO THE DINOSAURS?

66 million years ago, a large **asteroid** hit Earth at incredibly high speed. It caused a lot of fires and sent huge waves crashing across the land. Dust from the asteroid affected the weather and reduced the amount of food that the dinosaurs had to eat.

This made most dinosaurs become **extinct** – except for those that could fly, which survived and developed into the birds that we are familiar with today!

Archaeopteryx is described as the "missing link" between dinosaurs and birds!

## WHAT ARE FOSSILS?

**Fossils** are the remains of animals and plants that have been preserved for millions of years. They have been found on all seven of Earth's **continents**! Fossils of a dinosaur's entire **skeleton** are very rare. But even if they are found in bits and pieces, fossils allow scientists to learn a lot about the dinosaurs and their lives!

So far, only one Pegomastax fossil has been found!

# TYPES OF DINOSAURS

**Scientists have arranged the dinosaurs into different categories based on things that they had in common, like their size or the way that they walked.**

## THEROPODS

Theropods all walked on two legs. Smaller theropods often had feathers, while larger ones were some of the biggest meat-eaters ever!

## PACHYCEPHALOSAURS

These dinosaurs also walked on two legs. They are best known, however, for having very tough skulls!

## CERATOPSIANS

These plant-eating dinosaurs had large eye-catching frills on their heads that could be used for protection. Their frills also helped them to keep warm in cold weather.

## ORNITHOPODS

Ornithopods included several dinosaurs with duck-like beaks and crests on their heads. They were all plant-eaters rather than meat-eaters.

## SAUROPODS

Sauropods included some of the largest dinosaurs to ever walk the Earth! They are easy to identify because they all had very long necks and tails, with incredibly small heads in comparison.

## STEGOSAURS

Stegosaurs walked on four legs. Their most iconic features are the incredibly tough plates that ran across their backs and provided them with protection.

## ANKYLOSAURS

Like stegosaurs, ankylosaurs had protective plates across their bodies. Ankylosaurs, however, had much shorter legs and often had tails that were shaped like clubs.

## PTEROSAURS

These reptiles were close cousins of the dinosaurs and were the first animals after insects to develop the ability to fly. The very biggest had a similar wingspan to a small plane!

# FUNKY-FEATURED DINOSAURS

**Dinosaurs came in all shapes and sizes, but some had funky features that set them apart from the rest. Some made loud trumpeting noises to communicate with one another. Others were covered in spikes like a hedgehog! The dinosaurs in this book used their unusual features to help them survive in their prehistoric world.**

No front teeth!

# Muttaburrasaurus

One of this dinosaur's defining features was its large, rounded snout. It may have developed this for two reasons. The first is that it may have made Muttaburrasaurus's sense of smell stronger. The second is that it could have allowed it to make loud calling sounds to communicate with other dinosaurs.

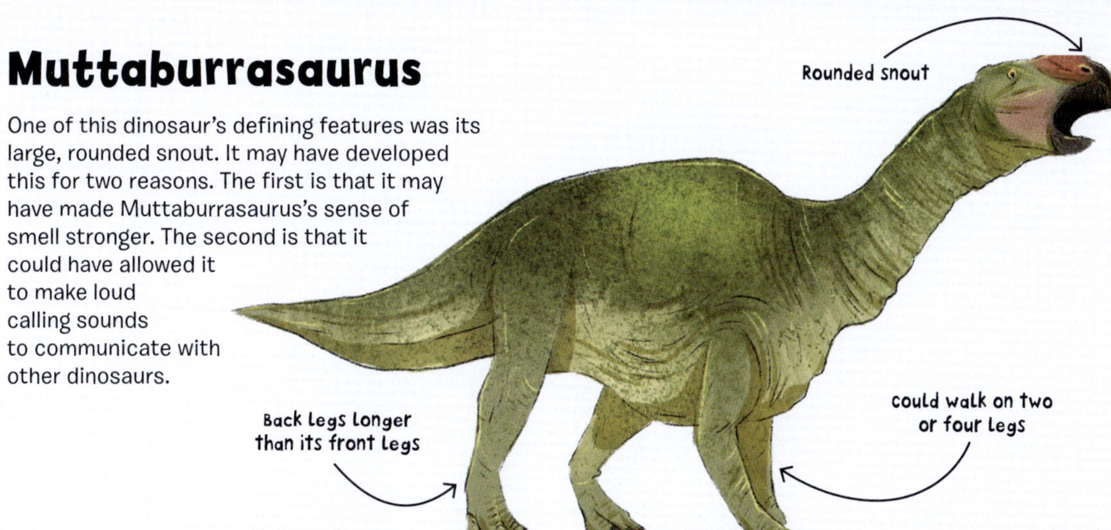


| | |
|---|---|
| **PRONUNCIATION:** MUT-a-BURR-a-SORE-us | **SIZE** |
| **DIET: Herbivore** | **SPEED** |
| **TIME PERIOD:** Early **Cretaceous** | **DEADLY RATING** |

# Nigersaurus

Nigersaurus had an incredible 500 teeth, a mixture of visible teeth and ones hidden away to be used as replacements. That's more teeth than any other dinosaur! It used them to munch on lots and lots of **vegetation**, and has been referred to as the "lawnmower" of the dinosaur world!

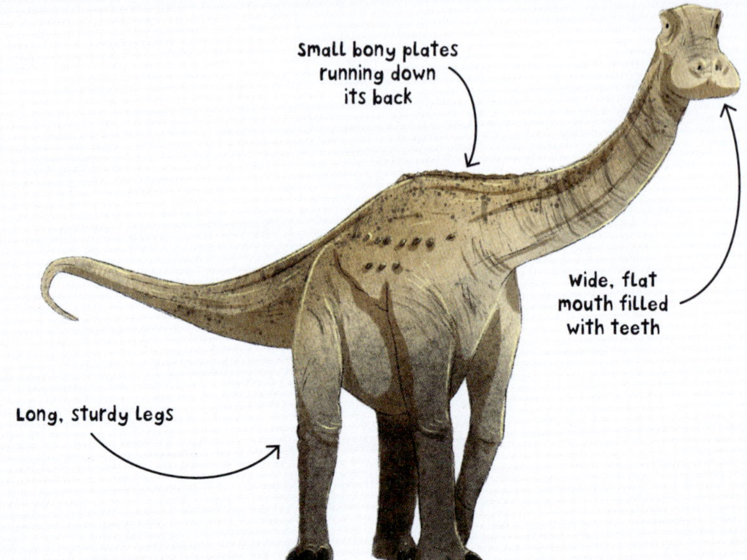


| | |
|---|---|
| **PRONUNCIATION:** ni-jer-SORE-us | **SIZE** |
| **DIET:** Herbivore | **SPEED** |
| **TIME PERIOD:** Early Cretaceous | **DEADLY RATING** |

# Yanornis

Yanornis may look a lot like a modern bird, but unlike the birds we know today it had lots of sharp teeth! While it mainly preferred to eat fish, it did occasionally switch its diet based on the food available around it.

Strong chest muscles

The size of a modern-day crow

Strong flyer

| | |
|---|---|
| **PRONUNCIATION:** yah-NOR-niss | **SIZE** |
| **DIET: Omnivore** | **SPEED** |
| **TIME PERIOD:** Early Cretaceous | **DEADLY RATING** |

# Gigantoraptor

The largest feathered dinosaur ever found, Gigantoraptor was over twice as tall as a human and almost the same length as a bus! This surprised scientists, as most feathered dinosaurs were very small. It also laid some of the largest dinosaur eggs ever found.

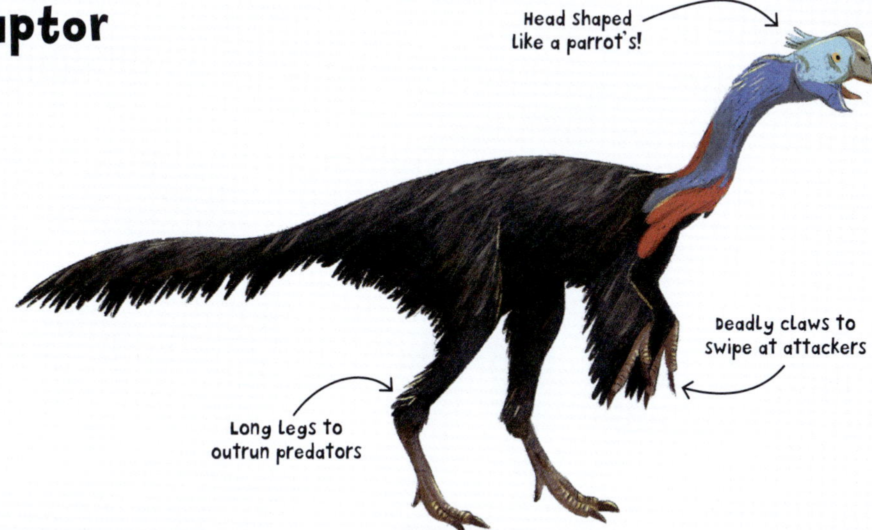


| | | |
|---|---|---|
| **PRONUNCIATION:** ji-GAN-to-rap-tor | **SIZE** | |
| **DIET:** Omnivore | **SPEED** | |
| **TIME PERIOD:** Late Cretaceous | **DEADLY RATING** | |

# Aquilarhinus

Duck-billed dinosaurs like Aquilarhinus were the most common plant-eating dinosaurs of their time. Their distinctive snouts and jaws were perfectly shaped to scoop up vegetation on the ground. Aquilarhinus also had a crest on its head, although it looked more like a humped nose!

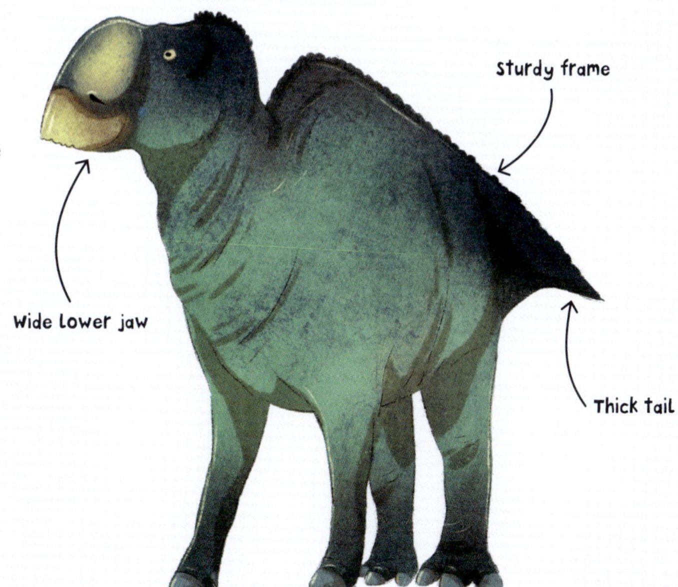


| | | |
|---|---|---|
| **PRONUNCIATION:** a-kwi-lar-EE-nuss | **SIZE** |   |
| **DIET:** Herbivore | **SPEED** |   |
| **TIME PERIOD:** Late Cretaceous | **DEADLY RATING** | |

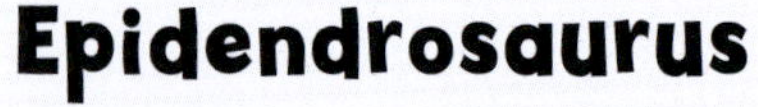

# Epidendrosaurus

The tiny Epidendrosaurus was a tree climber. It used its claws not only to grip onto tree trunks, but also to dig into tiny cracks to reach small insects. Scientists think that it would have been able to glide short distances from one branch to another.



**PRONUNCIATION:** epp-e-den-droh-SORE-us

**DIET:** Omnivore

**TIME PERIOD:** Mid **Jurassic**

SIZE

SPEED

DEADLY RATING

# Iguanodon

The second dinosaur to ever be discovered, Iguanodon had a large spike like a thumb on the end of its front legs. These could have been used to fight back against **predators** or to strip leaves from branches and make them easier to eat.



**PRONUNCIATION:** ig-WHA-noh-don

**DIET:** Herbivore

**TIME PERIOD:** Early Cretaceous

SIZE

SPEED

DEADLY RATING

## Anatotitan

Considering that its name means "duck titan", it's no surprise that Anatotitan was a duck-billed dinosaur. However, scientists think that it may actually be a fully-grown version of another dinosaur called Edmontosaurus rather than its own **species**!

| | |
|---|---|
| **PRONUNCIATION:** an-ah-toh-TIE-tan | SIZE |
| **DIET:** Herbivore | SPEED |
| **TIME PERIOD:** Late Cretaceous | DEADLY RATING |

## Oviraptor

The small Oviraptor spent a lot of its time crouching over its nest to look after its eggs and keep them warm. If any predator got too close, Oviraptor could protect them using its very sharp beak that was perfect for crushing things.

| | | |
|---|---|---|
| **PRONUNCIATION:** oh-vee-RAP-tor | SIZE |  |
| **DIET:** Omnivore | SPEED | |
| **TIME PERIOD:** Late Cretaceous | DEADLY RATING | |

# Pegomastax

This was a very unusual-looking dinosaur! Covered in spikes like a porcupine, Pegomastax had a short beak like a parrot's, and a pair of fang-like canine teeth. It was very rare for a herbivore to have such big canines! Pegomastax used them to defend itself or to fight other dinosaurs of the same species, rather than to eat meat.

Skull no longer than a pencil!

Blunt beak the perfect shape for picking fruit

Weighed less than a housecat!

| | |
|---|---|
| **PRONUNCIATION:** PEG-oh-mas-taks | **SIZE** 1/5 |
| **DIET:** Herbivore | **SPEED** 3/5 |
| **TIME PERIOD:** Early Jurassic | **DEADLY RATING** 2/5 |

Only one fossil has
ever been found!

# Heterodontosaurus

Heterodontosaurus is mostly known for having three different kinds of teeth. These teeth allowed it to tear, bite, and grind its food. It also had large cheek pouches to store food in while chewing so that nothing fell out!

Long, flexible tail
Five claws on each front foot

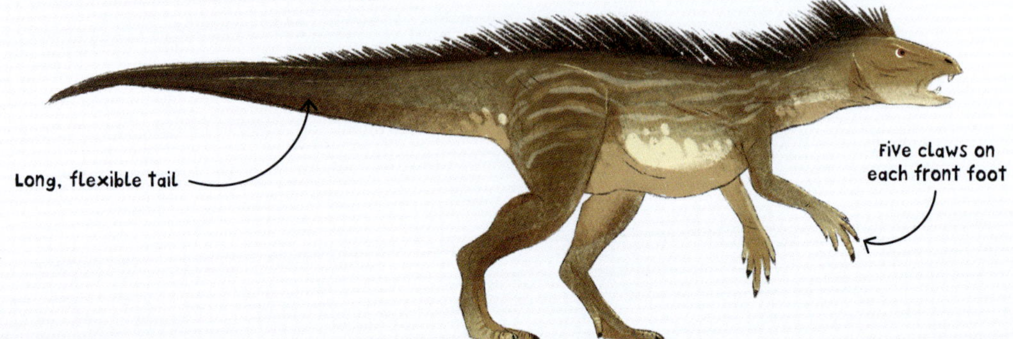

**PRONUNCIATION:** het-er-oh-DONT-oh-sore-us

**DIET:** Herbivore

**TIME PERIOD:** Early Jurassic

**SIZE**

**SPEED**

**DEADLY RATING**

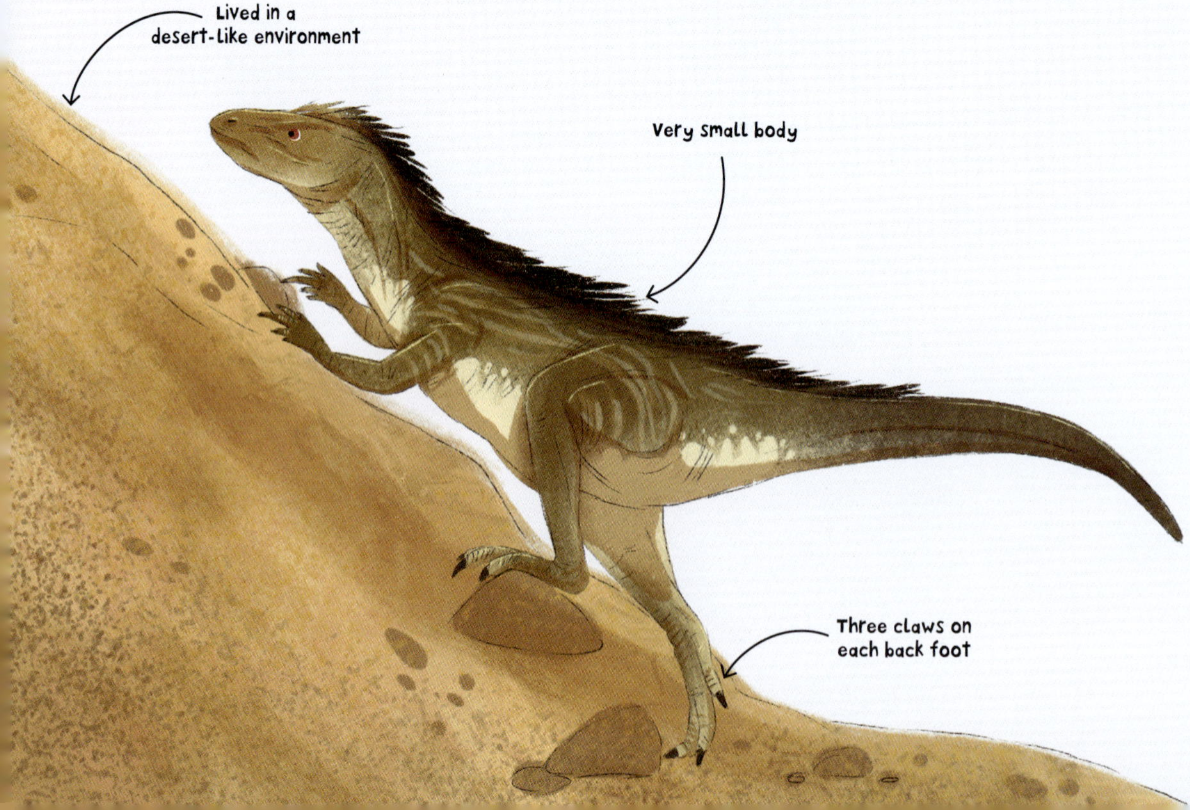
Lived in a desert-like environment
Very small body
Three claws on each back foot

# Sinosauropteryx

Sinosauropteryx was the first feathered dinosaur discovered that wasn't related to modern-day birds! It was also the first dinosaur that scientists were able to confidently say what color it was!

| | |
|---|---|
| **PRONUNCIATION:** sine-oh-SORE-op-ter-iks | **SIZE** |
| **DIET: Carnivore** | **SPEED** |
| **TIME PERIOD:** Early Cretaceous | **DEADLY RATING** |

# Stegosaurus

Stegosaurus is famous for the double row of triangle-shaped plates that ran along its back. These might have had two purposes. They could have been used to protect its spine and back. Alternatively, they could have acted like a radiator, soaking up sunlight to help keep Stegosaurus warm.

Spiky tail for swinging at predators

Small head with an even smaller brain

Front legs shorter than its back legs

| | |
|---|---|
| **PRONUNCIATION:** STEG-oh-SORE-us | **SIZE**  |
| **DIET:** Herbivore | **SPEED**  |
| **TIME PERIOD:** Late Jurassic | **DEADLY RATING** |

# Nothronychus

Nothronychus was a large dinosaur that usually preferred to eat plants. But its family tree shows that this might not have always been the case. Its close relatives were all carnivores, suggesting that Nothronychus changed its diet over time.



| | | | |
|---|---|---|---|
| **PRONUNCIATION:** noh-THRON-ee-kus | | **SIZE** | 3 of 5 |
| **DIET:** Omnivore | | **SPEED** | 3 of 5 |
| **TIME PERIOD:** Late Cretaceous | | **DEADLY RATING** | 3 of 5 |

# Giraffatitan

Compared to its close relatives, Giraffatitan had a shorter, thicker tail and a slimmer body. But it still had the classic long neck that made it look like, well, a giraffe!

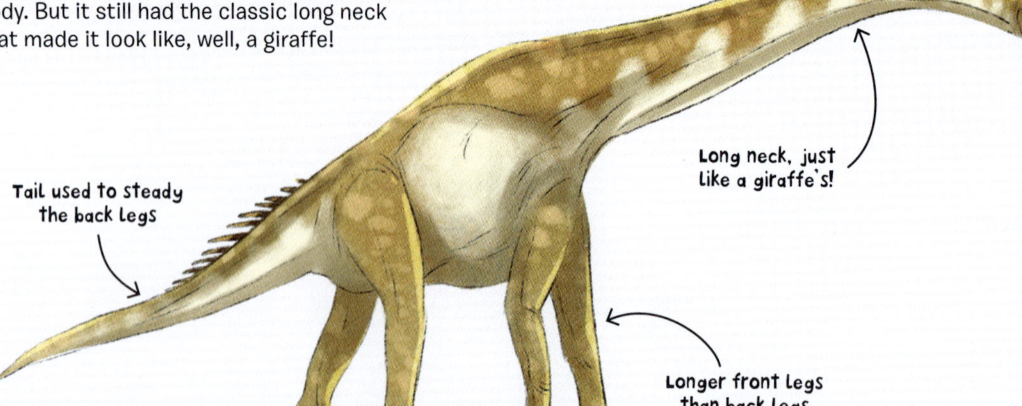


| | | | |
|---|---|---|---|
| **PRONUNCIATION:** ji-raf-a-TIE-tan | | **SIZE** | 5 of 5    |
| **DIET:** Herbivore | | **SPEED** | 1 of 5  |
| **TIME PERIOD:** Late Jurassic | | **DEADLY RATING** | 2 of 5 |

# Gryposaurus

A giant even compared to other duck-billed dinosaurs, Gryposaurus was the largest dinosaur living in its area. It had over 300 teeth that were perfect for eating almost any plants that it came across.

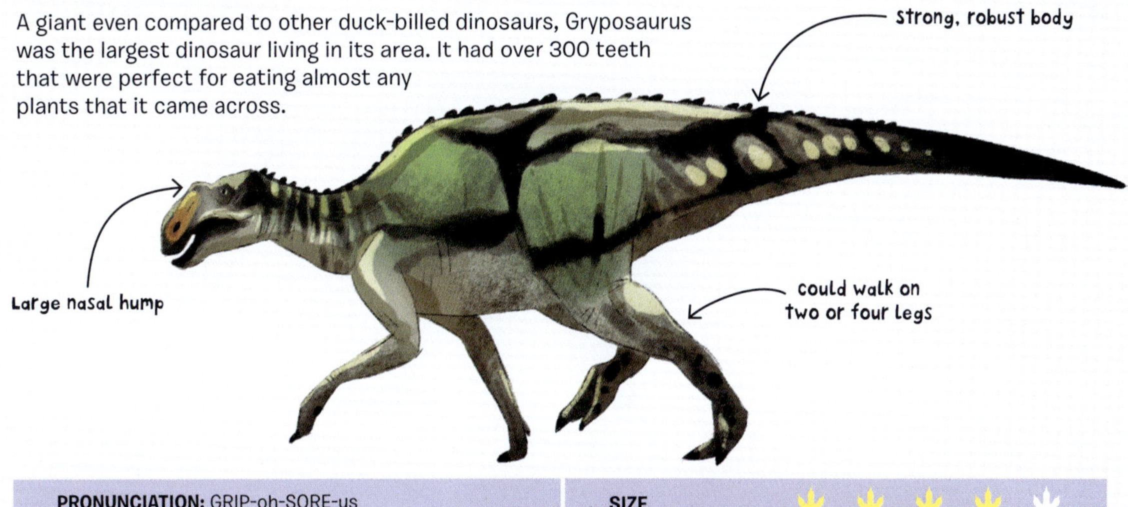


| | |
|---|---|
| **PRONUNCIATION:** GRIP-oh-SORE-us | **SIZE** |
| **DIET:** Herbivore | **SPEED** |
| **TIME PERIOD:** Late Cretaceous | **DEADLY RATING** |

# Anchiornis

Although it has been called "the earliest bird", Anchiornis was still a dinosaur – the oldest one able to glide, in fact! It shows that some dinosaurs grew feathers and other bird-like features long before true birds developed.

| | |
|---|---|
| **PRONUNCIATION:** an-kee-OR-niss | **SIZE** |
| **DIET:** Carnivore | **SPEED** |
| **TIME PERIOD:** Late Jurassic | **DEADLY RATING** |

# Corythosaurus

Corythosaurus used the crescent-shaped crest on its head to help produce sounds to communicate with other dinosaurs. It's also possible that the crest was used to control its body temperature or to attract a **mate**.

| | | |
|---|---|---|
| **PRONUNCIATION:** koh-rith-OH-sore-us | **SIZE** | |
| **DIET:** Herbivore | **SPEED** | |
| **TIME PERIOD:** Late Cretaceous | **DEADLY RATING** | |

# Rhinorex

Unlike its closest relatives, Rhinorex didn't have a crest on its head. Instead, it had an enormous nose! Unfortunately this didn't mean it had a better sense of smell. Instead, it was used to attract other Rhinorex or to help break up vegetation when eating.

| | | |
|---|---|---|
| **PRONUNCIATION:** RY-noh-rex | **SIZE** | |
| **DIET:** Herbivore | **SPEED** |   |
| **TIME PERIOD:** Late Cretaceous | **DEADLY RATING** | |

## Suzhousaurus

Suzhousaurus was part of a group of dinosaurs known for their extremely long claws. While it didn't have the longest claws of all, Suzhousaurus was still very impressive. It would have used its claws to reach above it and grab branches to eat from.

Small head

Wide body

Huge arms with enormous claws

| | | | |
|---|---|---|---|
| **PRONUNCIATION:** su-zoo-SORE-us | | **SIZE** | |
| **DIET:** Herbivore | | **SPEED** | |
| **TIME PERIOD:** Early Cretaceous | | **DEADLY RATING** | |

## Concavenator

Concavenator had two tall bones on its spine that gave it an unusual appearance. Whether these bones would have looked like a short, thin **sail** or like a camel's hump is a mystery to scientists – as is the reason why Concavenator had it in the first place!

| | | | |
|---|---|---|---|
| **PRONUNCIATION:** kon-ka-VEN-at-or | | **SIZE** |  |
| **DIET:** Carnivore | | **SPEED** | |
| **TIME PERIOD:** Early Cretaceous | | **DEADLY RATING** |  |

## Mosasaurus

The sleek and streamlined Mosasaurus was among the ocean's deadliest hunters. It used a snake-like movement of its body to push itself through the water in search of prey. It had no predators and wasn't picky about its food – it would eat anything that it came across!

**PRONUNCIATION:** moh-suh-SORE-us

**DIET:** Carnivore

**TIME PERIOD:** Late Cretaceous

| | |
|---|---|
| SIZE | 4/5 |
| SPEED | 3/5 |
| DEADLY RATING | 4/5 |

## Qianzhousaurus

Qianzhousaurus was a small, light theropod. It had a distinctive nose that was thin and long, giving it the nickname "Pinocchio rex". Because of this, it likely wouldn't have hunted or eaten in the same way as some of its bigger relatives, but it was still an intimidating predator!

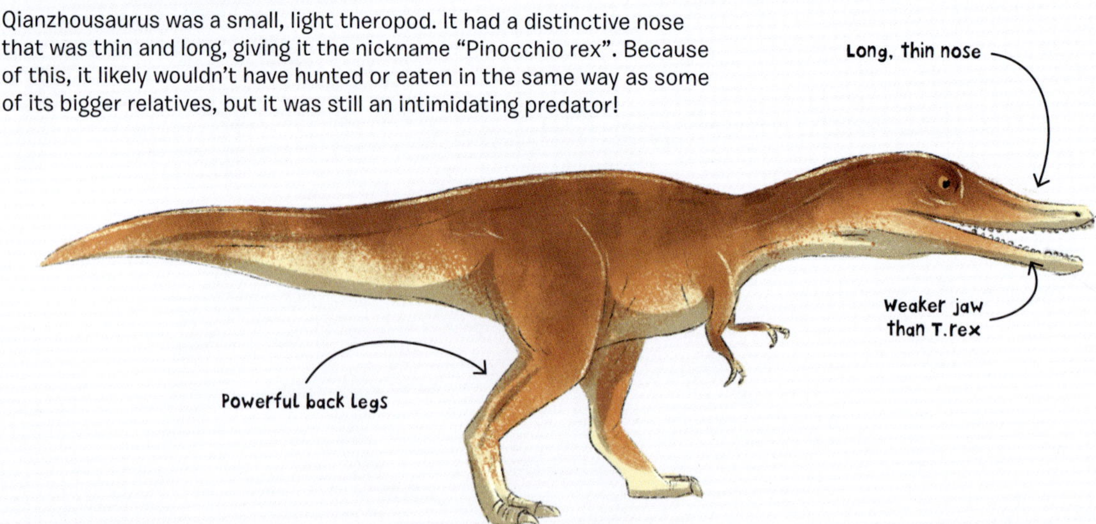


**PRONUNCIATION:** key-an-zoo-SORE-us

**DIET:** Carnivore

**TIME PERIOD:** Late Cretaceous

| | |
|---|---|
| SIZE | 3/5 |
| SPEED | 3/5 |
| DEADLY RATING | 3/5 |

## Incisivosaurus

The tiny Incisivosaurus may have been related to very large, fearsome meat-eaters, but besides walking on two legs it had very little in common with them! Incisivosaurus's teeth – including two very large front teeth – suggested that it was a plant-eater instead.

**PRONUNCIATION:** in-SIZ-oh-voe-SORE-us

**DIET:** Herbivore or omnivore

**TIME PERIOD:** Early Cretaceous

**SIZE**

**SPEED**

**DEADLY RATING**

## Parasaurolophus

This dinosaur is best known for the long, **hollow**, backward-curving crest on its head. Scientists believe that Parasaurolophus could blow air through it to create a loud trumpeting sound to communicate with other dinosaurs of the same species.

**PRONUNCIATION:** pa-ra-saw-ROL-off-us

**DIET:** Herbivore

**TIME PERIOD:** Late Cretaceous

**SIZE**   

**SPEED**

**DEADLY RATING**

# DID YOU KNOW?

**What more is there to know about these funky-featured dinos? Let's take a look at some amazing facts and find out!**

Thousands of Mosasaur fossils have been discovered across all the continents. There are about 40 different types of Mosasaurs known so far.

Young dinosaurs grew incredibly fast, reaching their full adulthood by around 8 years old - including the Stegosaurus.

The Muttaburrasaurus is one of the most complete dinosaurs from Australia, meaning that almost every part of its skeleton has been found. It was also the first Australian dinosaur to be put up for display.

Parasaurolophus likely lived in herds of up to 50, like modern cows.

Some scientists believe that the Giraffatitan's nostrils were on the top of its head and may have had trunks like elephants to reach even higher trees.

Some scientists think Nigersaurus may have had nearly 360-degree vision because its eyes were high on its head, helping it watch for predators while it ate plants.

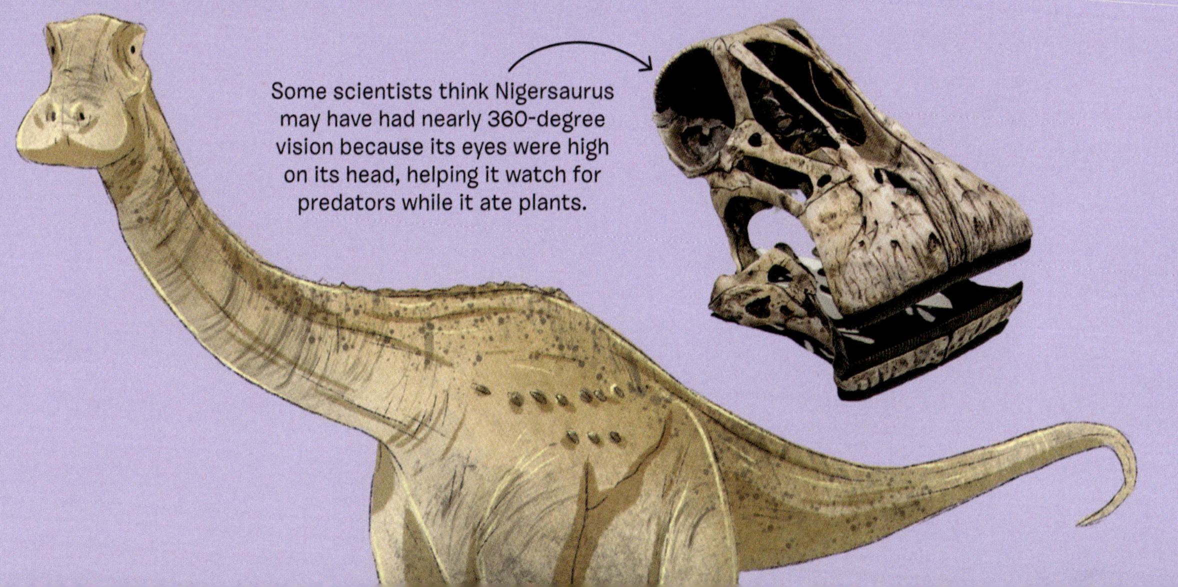

# NAME THAT DINO

**Can you name the dinosaur in the picture? Clues have been provided for you based on facts in the book.**

CLUE: These dinos had large front teeth, like a rabbit.

CLUE: These dinos had a mysterious bump on their back – whether it would have looked more like a short sail or camel's hump is a mystery!

CLUE: These dinos had incredibly large noses and weighed as much as an elephant.

CLUE: These dinos had a double row of triangle-shaped plates that ran along their backs.

CLUE: These dinos had very sharp beaks perfect for crushing things, but had no teeth!

CLUE: This dino's name means "duck titan."

CLUE: Only one fossil of this dino has ever been found, and scientists believe it was covered in spikes like a porcupine.

CLUE: These dinos were the first feathered dinosaur that weren't related to modern-day birds.

CLUE: These dinos belonged to a group that were known for their huge arms with enormous claws.

CLUE: These dinos were some of the deadliest ocean hunters, and would eat anything.

Answers can be found on page 32.

# WEIRD AND WACKY

**Dinosaurs weren't the only creatures on Earth millions of years ago. The world was full of strange plants, giant bugs, mysterious reptiles, and more! Let's meet some other prehistoric animals.**

## Giant Dragonfly: **Meganeura**

This enormous insect looked like a modern dragonfly, but it had a wingspan as wide as a seagull's! It lived in ancient forests and used its strong jaws to snap up smaller bugs.

## Sea Monster: **Elasmosaurus**

Elasmosaurus wasn't a dinosaur, it was a marine reptile! With a neck as long as a bus, it swam through ancient oceans using four paddle-shaped flippers. It may have snatched fish from the water's surface with its tiny head and super-stretchy neck.

## Armored Crocodile: **Desmatosuchus**

This odd-looking reptile had a body like a crocodile, a tiny head, and giant spikes on its shoulders. It trundled through swamps and plains, using its heavy armor to stay safe from predators. Scientists think it might have eaten plants!

## The Living Fossil: **Horseshoe Crabs**

Despite their name, horseshoe crabs are actually more closely related to scorpions and spiders than to crabs. Not only did they appear 200 million years before the first dinosaurs, they also survived the asteroid impact that caused the dinosaurs to become extinct. They still live on Earth today!

## Fish with Teeth: **Xiphactinus**

Xiphactinus was a fish longer than a human adult! It had a huge mouth full of sharp teeth and could gulp down prey almost its own size. Fossil evidence shows some even swallowed other fish whole!

# GLOSSARY

**Asteroid** – small, rocky objects that orbit the Sun.

**Carnivore** – an animal that only eats meat.

**Continents** – the huge pieces of land on Earth. For example, Africa and North America are separate continents.

**Cretaceous** – a period of time that lasted from about 143 to 66 million years ago.

**Extinct** – a species (see right) of animals with no living members.

**Fossils** – the remains or impression of plants and animals that lived long ago.

**Herbivore** – an animal that only eats plants.

**Hollow** – something that has an empty space inside.

**Jurassic** – a period of time that lasted from about 201 to 143 million years ago.

**Mate** – two animals that come together to produce young.

**Omnivore** – an animal that eats both plants and meat.

**Predators** – animals that hunt and kill other animals for food.

**Prehistoric** – the time before humans existed.

**Prey** – an animal that is hunted by other animals for food.

**Reptiles** – a group of cold-blooded animals, including snakes, lizards, crocodiles, and some types of dinosaurs.

**Sail** – a large, flat structure that grows on the backs of certain animals, including some dinosaurs.

**Skeleton** – the bony frame that supports and protects the body of a person or animal.

**Species** – a group of living things that share characteristics and features, and can produce young with each other. For example, Stegosaurus and Triceratops are different dinosaur species.

**Vegetation** - plant life in a particular area.

# INDEX

## NAME THAT DINO ANSWERS

1 - Incisivosaurus
2 - Concavenator
3 - Rhinorex
4 - Stegosaurus
5 - Oviraptor
6 - Anatotitan
7 - Pegomastax
8 - Sinosauropteryx
9 - Suzhousaurus
10 - Mosasaurus

## ABOUT THE AUTHOR

Rosie Rowntree is a children's author living in the west of Cornwall. Sharing her love of learning through her writing, she is passionate about sparking curiosity in children as they begin to broaden their horizons and learn about their surroundings - and beyond!

## ABOUT THE ILLUSTRATOR

Marina Halak is a talented illustrator of children's books from Ukraine. Her stunning illustrations are inspired by her own childhood, children, nature, magical moments and fairy tales. Marina is also the illustrator behind the related series, *Dogs* and *Cats*.

Picture Credits:
(abbreviations: t=top, b=bottom, m=middle, l=left, r=right)

Wikipedia: By Sculpture by Tyler Keillor and original photography by Ximena Erickson; image modified by Bonnie Miljour - Benton MJ (2010) Studying Function and Behavior in the Fossil Record. PLoS Biol 8(3): e1000321. doi:10.1371/journal.pbio.1000321.g001, CC BY 2.5, https://commons.wikimedia.org/w/index.php?curid=9624022 29mr.

Shutterstock: Barbara Ash 24tm; Catmando 29tr (desmatosuchus); Daniel Eskridge 25tr; Esteban De Armas 29br; Four Oaks 25ml; Jarous 29ml; life_in_a_pixel 28tl; Shvoeva Elena 24mr; SouthWestImagesAus 24bm; Suzi44 28br; THP Creative 29tr (scenery); William Cushman 25br.

Every effort has been made to trace the copyright holders, and we apologize in advance for any unintentional omissions. We would be pleased to insert the appropriate acknowledgments in any subsequent edition of this publication.